20.95

20.95

Humanitarian Organizations

Amnesty International

Ann Parry

CHELSEA HOUSE
PUBLISHERS
A Haights Cross Communications Company ®
Philadelphia

For Jack and Win Parry—exceptional and loving parents.

This edition first published in 2006 in the United States of America by Chelsea House Publishers, a subsidiary of Haights Cross Communications.

A Haights Cross Communications Company ®

Chelsea House Publishers
2080 Cabot Boulevard West, Suite 201
Langhorne, PA 19047-1813

The Chelsea House world wide web address is www.chelseahouse.com

First published in 2005 by
MACMILLAN EDUCATION AUSTRALIA PTY LTD
627 Chapel Street, South Yarra 3141

Visit our website at www.macmillan.com.au

Associated companies and representatives throughout the world.

Library of Congress Cataloging-in-Publication Data applied for.
ISBN 0 7910 8813 8

Edited by Angelique Campbell-Muir and Anna Fern
Cover and text design by Raul Diche
Maps by Pat Kermode
Photo research by Legend Images

Printed in China

Acknowledgments
The author and publisher are grateful to Amnesty International for its assistance and advice in the preparation of this book.

The author and the publisher are also grateful to the following for permission to reproduce copyright material:

Cover photographs: Amnesty demonstrations in Sydney, courtesy of David Gray/Reuters/Picturemedia. Amnesty demonstrations in Tokyo, courtesy of Picture Media/Reuters/Kimimasa Mayama. Student letter writer, courtesy of Amnesty International Australia.

AAP/AP Photo/Jose Caruci, p. 7; AAP/AP Photo/Renzo Gostoli, p. 20; Jorge Uzon/AFP, p. 17; Amnesty International, pp. 5, 6, 30; Amnesty International Australia, pp. 4 (logo), 8, 10, 11, 14, 22, 23, 27; Amnesty International Australia/The Age/Sandy Scheltema, p. 18; Amnesty International Australia/Nauru Wire, p. 15; Australian Picture Library/Corbis, p. 9; Australian Red Cross, p. 4 (logo); Ewa Bajbak, p. 26 (both); Rosey Boehm, p. 29; Greenpeace, p. 4 (logo); Doctors Without Borders/Médecins Sans Frontières (MSF), p. 4 (logo); http://www.mvfr.org/mvfr_com/pdf/malo.pdf, p. 24; Samkelo Mokhine, p. 28; the Peace Corps, p. 4 (logo); Picture Media/Reuters/Yves Herman, p. 25; Picture Media/Reuters/Mike Hutchings, p. 19; Picture Media/Reuters/Kimimasa Mayama, pp. 1, 16; Picture Media/Reuters/POOL, p. 21; Save the Children, p. 4 (logo).

Please note
At the time of printing, the Internet addresses appearing in this book were correct. Owing to the dynamic nature of the Internet, however, we cannot guarantee that all these addresses will remain correct.

Contents

Glossary words

When a word is printed in **bold**, its meaning is included on that page. You can also look up its meaning in the Glossary on page 31.

What is a humanitarian organization?

Humanitarian organizations work to help solve problems in countries around the world, wherever there is a need for their help. They are sometimes called aid agencies, non-profit, or non-governmental organizations (NGOs). Some organizations, such as Greenpeace, work to protect the environment. Others, such as Amnesty International and the International Red Cross, work to protect people's **human rights**, or provide for their basic needs in times of conflict and disaster. Doctors Without Borders sends **volunteers** anywhere in the world to give medical help to people affected by disasters. Groups like Save the Children and Australian Volunteers International help rebuild communities that need food, education, and advice.

Some humanitarian organizations are given money by governments to help run their programs. They also work hard to collect enough money from the public to keep going. Some of their workers are volunteers and are not paid, while others work for a small wage.

The *Humanitarian Organizations* series focuses on six well-known organizations and explains how they help those in need around the world.

The Peace Corps

The Red Cross

Greenpeace

 Save the Children

Save the Children

Amnesty International

Doctors Without Borders

About Amnesty International

Amnesty International is an organization that works to promote and protect the human rights of people around the world. It is not connected to any political or religious group.

Amnesty International is working towards a world in which every person enjoys basic human rights. It investigates and takes action all over the world, wherever it believes human rights are being threatened.

Human rights standards

The **United Nations** adopted a set of international human rights standards, which are in the Universal Declaration of Human Rights. Human rights include the right to physical freedom, to express opinions, and to choose your own religion and government.

Amnesty International believes that people should not be **discriminated** against because of their race, religion, or political beliefs. It believes all people should be entitled to a fair trial if they are accused of committing a crime. It believes all people are entitled to basic food and shelter. It believes children should have special rights to protection, education, and medical treatment. They should also have time to play and not be forced to do adult work. Amnesty International believes that people everywhere should be treated with respect.

This is the logo for Amnesty International.

Did you know?

Amnesty International has over 1.8 million members in more than 150 countries.

History of Amnesty International

One of the first special international years declared by the United Nations was World Refugee Year, in 1961. In that year, London lawyer Peter Benenson read about a group of students in Portugal who were arrested and jailed for raising their glasses and drinking to "freedom" in a public restaurant. Benenson was so angry about this incident that he began a one-year campaign for their release called "Appeal for Amnesty 1961" in a British newspaper, the *London Observer*.

This article was published as part of the "Appeal for Amnesty" campaign.

"Appeal for Amnesty" campaign

The "Appeal for Amnesty" campaign was not just for the Portuguese students. Many people were in prison because they had expressed their beliefs, or because they came from a particular political, racial, religious, or national group. Benenson called these people **prisoners of conscience**. The *London Observer* published a front-page appeal explaining the term "prisoners of conscience." It asked people to send in information about prisoners around the world. The information was then used in a special edition containing prisoners' stories. The idea for this campaign was to use the publicity to shame governments into treating prisoners properly or releasing them.

Amnesty International is formed

The campaign grew enormously and spread to other countries. By the end of 1961, the organization known as Amnesty International had been formed. It took as its symbol a lighted candle surrounded by barbed wire. This represents all the prisoners that Amnesty International has not been able to help and also reminds people of the old Chinese saying: "Better to light a candle than curse the darkness." The saying means that it is better to take action to improve a situation than to just complain.

Glossary word

prisoners of conscience
people who have been put into prison purely for holding beliefs that powerful people disagree with

Did you know?

Diana Redhouse, a British member of Amnesty International, designed the original candle-in-barbed-wire logo in June 1961.

One former army general in Mexico received 50,000 letters from Amnesty International members during his 14 years as a prisoner of conscience.

Letter-writing campaigns

Amnesty International's earliest activity was letter writing. Before beginning a campaign, though, Amnesty International would investigate a prisoner's case and decide if he or she really was a "prisoner of conscience." If they were, Amnesty International would "adopt" this prisoner. Members would write numerous letters to officials in that country asking for the release of that prisoner. Sometimes, if it was safe to do so, members would also contact the prisoner's family and offer help.

Crowds of music fans at a concert in Venezuela which was held at the Caracas airfield on July 19, 1998, as part of a human rights campaign sponsored by Amnesty International.

Adoption groups

Later, Amnesty International members formed what they called "adoption groups." These groups worked together on particular campaigns, or tried to free prisoners in particular countries. The groups also helped with publicity, education, and fundraising. They contacted schools, churches, business groups, and **unions**. This brought in many new members and resources.

In the late 1960s, Amnesty International decided that groups should only work on cases outside of their own country. This distance prevented them from taking sides while collecting information. It also helped to protect members from being threatened by the people who were holding the prisoners.

Greater public awareness

In 1977, Amnesty International was awarded the **Nobel Prize for Peace** for its work. In the 1980s, famous artists and musicians helped to publicize Amnesty International. They made more people around the world aware of the organization and what it was trying to do. They also raised a lot of money. Amnesty International used the money to open new offices around the world and was able to help more prisoners than ever before.

Glossary words

unions
associations of workers that fight for better pay and conditions

Nobel Prize for Peace
an award presented by the Nobel Committee in Sweden to a person or group who gives the greatest benefit to humankind

The founder of Amnesty International

Peter Benenson was born in England in 1921. While attending school, he studied history and law, and joined the Labour Party. But he began fighting against injustice long before that. While at boarding school, he wrote a letter to his headmaster complaining about the food. By the age of 16, Benenson was working to help victims of the Spanish **Civil War**, and sent money to support one of the orphaned babies.

Working for better systems of justice

In the early 1950s, Benenson went to Spain as an observer in the trials of unionists. At this time he began to work for better systems of justice in countries such as Hungary and South Africa. In 1961, Benenson formed Amnesty International.

Amnesty International criticized the unjust treatment of prisoners in countries around the world. It caused great controversy and was attacked by foreign governments.

Benenson retires

In 1966, Benenson temporarily retired from the organization he had founded. In the mid-1980s he returned to Amnesty International as a speaker and campaigner.

In a 2001 television broadcast to nine million people, Benenson received a Pride of Britain Lifetime Award. He accepted it on behalf of Amnesty International.

In 1991, Peter Benenson lit a candle to commemorate the organization he founded 30 years earlier.

Did you know?

In the 1990s, Peter Benenson was working to rescue orphans in Romania. By this time he was in his seventies.

Glossary words

civil war
war between different groups within a country

Early work

First prisoners of conscience

The first prisoners of conscience that Amnesty International campaigned for were Constantin Noica and the Reverend Ashton Jones.

Constantin Noica

Noica taught at a university in Romania. As a punishment for having different ideas than the government, he was suspended from his job. His friends and pupils continued to visit him and listen to his opinions. When the government found out about this, they sentenced Noica to 25 years in prison in 1958. Noica was eventually released in 1964, after Amnesty International took up his case.

Did you know?

Amnesty International began its first "Christmas card action" in 1961. The cards listed the names of 12 prisoners of conscience to publicize their cases.

Reverend Ashton Jones

In 1960, there was a campaign in the southern part of the United States of America to give African–Americans the same rights as white Americans. The Reverend Ashton Jones was one of the leaders of this campaign. Jones was beaten and imprisoned several times before Amnesty International began to protest on his behalf. He was eventually freed.

First "urgent action"

The first "urgent action" taken by Amnesty International was for Professor Luiz Basilio Rossi in 1973. Professor Rossi had been arrested in Brazil for his political beliefs. Rossi believes that once his case was made public by Amnesty International, the Brazilian government took more care to treat him reasonably in prison. Professor Rossi was eventually released on bail and fled to Belgium.

Protestors march for equal rights for African–Americans in the United States of America in the 1960s.

Core values of Amnesty International

Core values are the things that a person, group, or organization really believes in. The values are used to work out rules of behavior. Amnesty International is a worldwide group of human rights defenders. Its core values include:

Solidarity and global coverage

Amnesty International thinks that people of all countries need to work together, to make a strong voice that can be heard everywhere.

Specific actions to help individual victims

Amnesty International believes that all basic human rights should belong to all people—not just some rights for some people.

Independence

Amnesty International does not accept money or other support from any government. It must remain completely independent to effectively fight against human rights abuses.

Democracy

Amnesty International thinks that all people should be able to participate in government, for example, by having the right to vote. It believes that democracy and human rights should be the basis of all cultures and societies.

Respect

Amnesty International considers that people everywhere should treat each other with respect.

Did you know?

North Korea is reported to have between 150,000 and 200,000 political prisoners working as slave laborers in prison colonies.

Amnesty International launched its global campaign to "Stop Violence Against Women" at an international meeting in Mexico.

How Amnesty International works

Amnesty International works with many other groups around the world. They work with governments, groups that work between governments (such as the United Nations), political groups, and businesses. Members of Amnesty International try to warn these groups, and the general public, about abuses of human rights.

What Amnesty International workers do

Amnesty International workers do a lot of research on individual victims and cases where there seems to be a pattern of abuses of people's rights. Once the organization believes it has accurate information, it publicizes the story. Then members, supporters, and staff organize public pressure on governments and others to stop the abuses. Amnesty International is careful to check all the facts, to get the news out quickly, and to keep up the publicity until it gets results.

The rule of law and human rights standards

As well as working on individual cases of human rights abuse, Amnesty International also works to convince all governments around the world to respect the rule of law and to have good human rights standards.

Amnesty International carries out a wide range of human rights educational activities. Through these activities it encourages all sorts of organizations and individuals to support and respect human rights.

Did you know?

Amnesty International has found that 4,500 children are currently in **detention** in Pakistan. Most have not even been convicted of any crime.

Glossary word

detention
a type of
imprisonment

An Amnesty International member talks to a group of students about human rights.

11

Where in the world is Amnesty International?

Amnesty International works in many countries around the world. This map shows where Amnesty International is represented by offices.

Timeline

Amnesty International has been working to help people since it began in 1961.

1961	Amnesty International is founded by Peter Benenson. The candle-and-barbed-wire logo is designed.
1962	Amnesty International undertakes its first mission, to Ghana. 210 prisoners of conscience are adopted by 70 groups in seven different countries.
1963	Amnesty International grows to 350 groups. 140 of the 770 prisoners of conscience adopted in Amnesty's first two years are released.
1965	Amnesty International issues its first reports, on prison conditions in Portugal, South Africa, and Romania.
1972	Amnesty International launches its first worldwide campaign for the abolition of torture.
1977	Amnesty International wins Nobel Prize for Peace.
1985	Amnesty International expands its work to include help for refugees and publishes its first educational pack, "Teaching and Learning About Human Rights."
1988	Amnesty International's "Human Rights Now!" concert, to celebrate the 40th anniversary of the Universal Declaration of Human Rights, tours to 19 cities in 15 countries, and leads to a dramatic increase in Amnesty International's membership.
1990	There are now 700,000 Amnesty International members in 150 countries.
1992	Amnesty International has more than one million members, including more than 6,000 local groups in 70 countries.
1996	Amnesty International campaigns for a permanent International Criminal Court to bring to justice the perpetrators of the worst human rights abuses. Two years later, this court is established by a United Nations Diplomatic Conference.
2004	Amnesty International expands its work on economic, social, and cultural rights, and launches a new global campaign to "Stop Violence Against Women."

Key to countries

PACIFIC REGION
Australia, New Zealand

ASIA AND THE MIDDLE EAST
Hong Kong, India, Israel, Japan, Jordan, Kuwait, Malaysia, Mongolia, Nepal, Pakistan, Palestinian Authority, Philippines, Thailand

EUROPE
Austria, Belarus, Belgium, Croatia, Czech Republic, Denmark, Faroe Islands, Finland, France, Germany, Greece, Hungary, Iceland, Ireland, Italy, Luxembourg, Moldova, Netherlands, Norway, Poland, Portugal, Russia, Slovak Republic, Slovenia, Spain, Sweden, Switzerland, Turkey, Ukraine, United Kingdom

AFRICA
Algeria, Benin, Burkina Faso, Côte d'Ivoire, Egypt, Gambia, Ghana, Mali, Mauritius, Morocco, Nigeria, Senegal, Sierra Leone, South Africa, Tanzania, Togo, Tunisia, Zambia, Zimbabwe

NORTH AND CENTRAL AMERICA
Aruba, Bahamas, Barbados, Bermuda, Canada, Costa Rica, Grenada, Jamaica, Mexico, Netherland Antilles, Puerto Rico, United States of America

SOUTH AMERICA
Argentina, Bolivia, Chile, Colombia, Ecuador, Guyana, Paraguay, Peru, Uruguay, Venezuela

Concerns, campaigns, and classic actions

Amnesty International is concerned about a range of problems throughout the world. It identifies specific campaigns and takes action accordingly.

CONCERNS

Torture

Amnesty International is concerned that in some countries, prisoners are deliberately tortured to make them confess to something or to give information about others.

CAMPAIGNS

Amnesty International has recorded examples of torture in more than 100 countries. When a case is confirmed, they act quickly and strongly. Within hours, a network of up to 75,000 people in over 70 countries can be notified to act. They send urgent faxes, letters, and emails to the authorities responsible. All their messages say the same thing: "Stop torture. Respect human rights." By having its members send these messages, Amnesty International gets results in roughly one-third of these sorts of cases every year.

Another important way of reducing occurrences of torture is by preventing torture equipment from being made and sold. Amnesty International has produced reports on this, and is campaigning for the passing of international laws to make the production and sale of torture items illegal.

Classic action

East Timor was **occupied** by Indonesia for 22 years. Many people who campaigned for independence were arrested. One of these was a young student who was repeatedly tortured by the secret police. After several weeks he was taken to the Commander's office and shown letters from complete strangers demanding his release. He was finally released.

This performance was part of the campaign for independence in East Timor, which was achieved in 1999.

Refugee rights

Amnesty is concerned that people all over the world have been forced to leave their countries in fear of their lives, or for social or economic reasons. Many of them suffer discrimination.

CAMPAIGNS

Refugees come from countries where their human rights have not been respected. It may have been that they could not follow their own religion, politics, or work without being punished or discriminated against. Many refugees find that when they arrive in a new country, they are seen as problems, or even as terrorists. Amnesty International campaigns to prevent refugees being forced back to their original country, where they may be tortured or killed. They believe that refugees have the right to be kept safe and treated with dignity until a long-term solution can be found for their situation.

Classic action

Many people fled from Afghanistan after recent wars. Although the country remains unsafe, many are being encouraged or even forced to return. Amnesty International has investigated the problems this has caused, and is now **lobbying** a number of countries as well as the United Nations on three issues:

- basic safety must be assured
- justice systems in Afghanistan such as police and courts must be working fairly
- reconstruction in Afghanistan must be more advanced.

Children are among the Afghan refugees being held in this detention center in Nauru.

Glossary word

lobbying
attempting to convince government, business, or other powerful groups to change their policy or practices

Prisoners of conscience

Amnesty International is concerned that current systems of justice are not always fair and equal for all people. In some countries, people are imprisoned for expressing their political or religious beliefs, or for a particular way of life. These people have committed no violent crimes, nor have they encouraged others to be violent.

CAMPAIGNS

Freedom of expression is an important human right. Amnesty International began with Peter Benenson's concern on this very issue. Since then, Amnesty International has campaigned for the immediate and unconditional release of many prisoners of conscience. Although not all are set free, many have still been helped by letter-writing campaigns. Some of these prisoners have reported that their treatment improved and that their jailers seemed more aware of human rights. This can be enough to keep the prisoner alive until the situation changes and they may eventually be released.

Classic action

Aung San Suu Kyi is a political leader in Burma (Myanmar), South-East Asia. Her party actually won the elections in 1990 but was prevented from taking power by the ruling military group. Since 1988 she has spent most of her time under house arrest, often in solitary confinement. Amnesty has sent researchers to Burma to investigate and visit political prisoners. They hope to influence the current government to release Aung San Suu Kyi unconditionally, and to convince them to **negotiate** the country's future with her.

This protest against Burma's military leaders took place in Tokyo, Japan, on September 1, 2003. Demonstrators are holding pictures of Aung San Suu Kyi.

Glossary word

negotiate
discuss, with the aim of reaching an agreement or compromise

Violence against women

Amnesty International is aware that the greatest threat to the human rights of many women is violence that occurs in their own homes. They are also concerned about the violence against women that happens during and after wars.

CAMPAIGNS

In 2004, Amnesty International began a new campaign to stop violence against women. Many women suffer and die each year because they are not given the same human rights as men. Women have been killed merely because they are working for women's rights. Others have been killed for simply leaving their home without a male escort from their family. Amnesty International calls for effective action to be taken by communities and governments against people using violence towards women. It believes that there needs to be programs for the protection of women and the prevention of future violence.

Classic action

In Cuidad Juarez, Mexico, more than 400 teenage girls have been murdered in the last ten years. The murders are not the result of a war or government action, but a terrible violation of the human rights of women. Young men have not been affected. Amnesty International has published a report urging the government to make themselves accountable for a proper investigation into these murders.

Amnesty International wants the Mexican government to investigate the murders of teenage girls.

Child soldiers

Amnesty International is concerned that nearly half a million children have been recruited into armed groups, often against their will, in more than 85 countries around the world.

Child soldiers are usually between 15 and 18 years old, but can be as young as 10 years old. Child soldiers are used by both government and opposition groups. They are provided with modern lightweight weapons so that they can become efficient killers. Child soldiers also serve as spies, messengers, **sentries**, **porters**, and servants. They are considered easier to train, and are sometimes drugged to make them more obedient.

Amnesty International works to build up international opinion against the use of child soldiers, and to develop agreements not to use them. It also campaigns against the selling and export of weapons such as grenades and small automatic weapons that can be used easily by these young soldiers.

Amnesty International wants to stop the use of child soldiers in places such as Thailand.

Classic action

"K…" has been a soldier in the Congo in Africa since he was nine years old. He has seen and done terrible things, including killing people and burning houses. Now he cannot sleep at night. He has lost his childhood and education. In 2002, Amnesty International helped to bring into force a **treaty** to ban the use of soldiers under the age of 18 years. While it is too late for "K…," this treaty may help others like him.

Glossary words

sentries
people, often military, who watch for intruders

porters
people employed to carry loads

treaty
formal signed agreement between states or countries

18

The death penalty

Amnesty International is concerned about the use of the death penalty, which it considers to be cruel and inhuman. The death penalty cannot be reversed. It violates the right to life and has not been shown to deter crime. It can kill innocent people.

CAMPAIGNS

Opposition to the death penalty has been part of Amnesty International's work since it began in 1961. It has worked with a variety of other groups and individuals for more than 40 years to eliminate this ultimate abuse of human rights.

Over the years, a lot of progress has been made. By 2003, 76 countries had abolished the death penalty completely, and 16 countries had banned it for all but exceptional crimes. Twenty other countries had a death penalty law, but were not using it.

Amnesty International continues to collect information on executions. It lobbies governments of countries such as China, Iran, and the United States of America, where the death penalty is still in use.

Classic action

Amina Lawal lives in Nigeria. In 2002, she was sentenced to death by stoning because she had a child while unmarried. The man said to be the child's father denied it, and was not charged. Amina's lawyers, Amnesty International, and other human rights groups fought against the death penalty. Over a year later, the Nigerian Court finally decided that the conviction was not legal, and Amina was freed.

Many people protested against the death sentence on Amina Lawal. These women were part of a campaign in Cape Town, South Africa.

Uncontrolled spread of arms

Amnesty International is concerned that trade in all kinds of weapons is nearly out of control. Guns, bombs, mines, and grenades are sold throughout the world. The sale of arms is fueling conflict, poverty, and human rights abuses around the world.

CAMPAIGNS

Every minute, arms are used to kill someone somewhere in the world. The money that is spent on arms in poor countries would often be enough to provide basic health care and education for the people of that country. Amnesty International, Oxfam, and the International Action Network on Small Arms are three international organizations that believe something can be done.

In 1997, a Landmines Treaty was brought in after worldwide pressure was put on governments. No country has openly traded in mines since. Amnesty International believes that a similar Arms Trade Treaty would limit the amount of arms being exported to countries where they can be used to violate human rights.

Classic action

In 2003, after five years of arguing, the Brazilian Congress passed a new law making it illegal for most civilians to carry firearms. This was unusual because many countries today still do not have such a law. In the near future, the people of Brazil will also vote on the issue of banning gun sales to civilians altogether. This is the kind of result that Amnesty International and other organizations are working for.

Around 10,000 firearms were collected and destroyed after the Brazilian Congress passed its historic law.

International justice

Amnesty International is concerned that human rights abuses will continue as long as there is not any lawful punishment. Amnesty International campaigned for many years for the establishment of a just, fair, and independent International Criminal Court (ICC).

CAMPAIGNS

Sometimes, particularly during wars, dreadful crimes are committed against soldiers and civilians. In the past, it has been very difficult to try the people responsible and to punish them. Amnesty International is working with thousands of people worldwide to change this. The ICC is the first-ever permanent international criminal court established to stop human rights abuses and to ensure that crimes do not go unpunished. Currently, 97 countries work with the court. Amnesty International is calling on all governments in the world to cooperate with the ICC so it can start working in the name of justice when national courts are unable or unwilling to do so.

United Nations guards with a Bosnian Serb, on trial at the International War Crimes Tribunal in the Hague.

Classic action

The United States of America is the only country that is actively opposed to the ICC. The United States has asked other countries not to give Americans up for trial for such things as war crimes. Amnesty International has organized a petition urging other countries not to agree to this.

The people of Amnesty International

Amnesty International helps people and communities all over the world. Here are four volunteers who use their own specialized skills to help in different situations.

RUSSELL THIRGOOD Lawyer and National President

As well as his role at Amnesty International, Russell Thirgood works as a lawyer for a large legal firm in Brisbane.

Russell first contacted Amnesty International in 1987 when he was only 12 years old. He asked for information about the death penalty for a school debate. Russell was so shocked and outraged by what he read that he has been involved in the organization ever since. Russell is currently the National President of Amnesty International Australia.

Russell has traveled the world in his work for human rights and has met many victims of discrimination and abuse. With Amnesty International, he fights to build a framework of legal protection to prevent the same treatment from happening to others. It can be frustrating at times, especially when things do not progress as fast as they should, and time begins to run out for those who need help. Mostly, though, Russell finds his volunteer work with Amnesty International exciting and rewarding. It is hard work, but it changes lives and helps to create a better world. Russell believes that he is giving something back in return for all the opportunities that life in Australia has provided for him.

Did you know?

Amnesty International celebrated its 40th anniversary in 2001.

Russell comes from a close family, including a grandmother who was herself a victim of human rights abuse during World War II. Russell recently managed to arrange **compensation** for her for what she had suffered, and was able to take her back to Europe to visit her sister after 60 years. His parents, partner, and two golden retriever puppies don't see as much of him as they would like, but they give him the support he needs to continue his work with Amnesty International.

People around the world already have great respect for the ways Amnesty International goes about its work. Russell would like to see the work continue to grow, and to produce even more positive results for the people the organization is trying to help. He believes that human rights are important because people are important.

Did you know?

The Tiger XI soccer team is made up of mainly Afghani refugees.

Russell says: "Human rights are simply about looking after people. It is about standing up to bullies and taking sides with the battler. We must be brave enough to look outside our own backyards and troubles and stand up for those who need a helping hand."

On Friday nights when he is home, Russell plays soccer with the Tiger XI team.

EVE MALO Death penalty activist

Activist Eve Malo believes that the death penalty is no solution to crime.

Since her childhood in Germany in the late 1930s, Eve Malo has been aware of injustice in the way humans treat each other. Feeling driven to try to fight for human rights, she joined Amnesty International in 1989.

During her time with Amnesty International, Eve Malo has been involved in campaigns for Native American rights, prisoner rights, anti-nuclear campaigns, and peace work.

Most recently she has become the death penalty coordinator for Montana in the United States of America. She had already been involved with Murder Victims' Families for Reconciliation, a group which campaigns against the death penalty, even though some of them have had a family member murdered.

Eve's first job as coordinator involved visiting a prisoner waiting to be executed. She had only visited a prison once before that, but has now been visiting and writing to this prisoner for many years, as his case drags on. By working with several human rights organizations, Eve has been part of the movement that convinced the government of Montana to forbid execution of criminals under the age of 18 years, even if they have committed a crime that usually would mean the death penalty.

Did you know?

The youngest child executed in the last six years was a 13 year old from Pakistan. The laws that allowed this to happen have since been changed.

Glossary word

activist
a person who takes direct action for a cause

These people are demonstrating against the death penalty, an abuse of human rights that does nothing to address the causes of crime and antisocial behavior.

One of the ways that Eve spread the anti-death-penalty message was to travel throughout her state in a sheep wagon to talk at public meetings. (A sheep wagon is like the covered wagons seen in old western movies.) With her friend, 80-year-old Clare Sinclair, Eve spoke to the families of people who had killed other people, and heard how their lives had been affected. Some had been treated as though they were guilty, too. Wherever Eve and Clare went, communities talked of preventing crime and having offenders take some action to make up for what they had done. No one was in favor of punishments and revenge that seemed to have no positive effects.

Eve has gone on to work on other projects as well. One is a book for young people about 10 winners of the Nobel Prize for Peace. Eve came up with the idea for the book while at a United Nations conference on women's issues in China.

Eve is also training to become a mediator for young people who have committed crimes. Her job will be to work with the offenders and the victims, and to help each of them come up with ways of restoration that will make both parties feel better.

Did you know?

In the United States of America, 107 prisoners who were due to be executed were later released after they were proven, in fact, to be innocent.

EWA BAJBAK Student activist

In her home country of Poland, Ewa Bajbak works to help educate young people about human rights issues.

Ewa Babjak joined Amnesty International when she was just 16 years old. Her mother, a primary-school teacher, had worked for Amnesty International in the past and Ewa believed she could also help. Before that, Ewa had spent two years as a volunteer in a Polish organization called the Committee for Protecting Children's Rights. Now she is 19 years old and attends the First High School in Poznan, Poland.

Ewa's main interest since joining Amnesty International is in the area of human rights education. She organizes meetings for teenagers where participants can learn about human rights. Ewa also prepares workshops to show young people how they can take some action to improve human rights, both in Poland and internationally.

A national trade union movement called Solidarity began in Poland in 1980. It was lead by Lech Walesa and marked the beginning of some major improvements in human rights. Nine years later, the first non-communist government in 40 years was formed. In 1990, Walesa became the first popularly elected president of Poland.

Eva helps to promote community awareness of Amnesty International's work.

Did you know?

A total of 27,708 letters were written by Polish activists during Amnesty International's 24-hour letter-writing marathon in 2003.

In 2002, Amnesty International began a 24-hour letter-writing marathon for young people in Poland. Groups were encouraged to get together for International Human Rights Day on December 10th and to spend 24 hours writing petitions, appeals to governments, and letters to prisoners. This action was so successful that it was repeated in 2003.

This student is writing letters in support of Amnesty International's "Stop Violence Against Women" campaign.

Ewa is involved in Amnesty International street actions, which take place about five times a year. She would also like to start a special team for children's rights in the Polish branch. She finds the work she does for Amnesty International very satisfying, but admits it is sometimes disappointing when it is not always possible to achieve everything she would like to. However, Ewa accepts that she can only keep on working and try to make as much difference as she can.

SAMKELO MOKHINE Press officer

Samkelo Mokhine works in a full-time job, as well as volunteering for Amnesty International.

Samkelo Mokhine is a volunteer media officer for Amnesty International and a chairman of their International Global Media Team. He joined Amnesty International in 1991, during his first year of college, and helped found the Johannesburg group. Samkelo's legal qualifications mean he also specializes in working on Amnesty International plans and policies.

Samkelo attends many meetings and travels regularly to other countries on humanitarian missions for Amnesty International. The most stressful one of these was in 2002, when he and another Amnesty International worker visited victims of human rights violations in Zimbabwe. They reassured the victims that the outside world would hear what was happening to them. Samkelo was so horrified by what he had heard that he regularly gave interviews on his cell phone to members of the media who had been banned by the government. Samkelo knew it was important to get the information out and felt this was something he just had to do, even though it put him in a very dangerous situation.

In September 2003, police closed the *Daily News* offices in Harare, Zimbabwe. They requested all staff to leave, and arrested the editor and the operations manager. The offices had been petrol-bombed three times since the paper was founded in 1999.

Amnesty International regularly criticizes the actions of governments around the world. This can be very dangerous work. In South Africa it led to threats being made against Samkelo and others, and increased activity by people thought to be foreign security agents. It is frightening for Samkelo's family and girlfriend, who worry when he has to go to troubled parts of the world. Fortunately they are very supportive, and understand that his work is important.

Samkelo hopes that Amnesty International will continue to grow. More members will give the organization an even bigger voice against violations of human rights. He knows from the people who congratulate him on the street that Amnesty's work is important, and that the victims of abuses believe the organization can help them. This gives Samkelo great satisfaction. He hopes that one day Amnesty International will only have to promote human rights and that actual violations will be a thing of the past.

Did you know?

Between March 2001 and March 2002, 214 incidents of deaths in custody and 371 deaths resulting from police action were investigated in South Africa. In a third of the cases that were fully investigated, it was recommended that the police officers involved be prosecuted.

Irene Khan, Amnesty International Secretary-General, works to bring international attention to violations of human rights in South Africa and elsewhere.

What can you do?

Amnesty International is active in education systems around the world, particularly in high schools, colleges, and universities. Group members regularly meet face-to-face to plan their activities, which might include campaigning, fundraising, and human rights promotion. School groups often specialize in mass actions and big events. These sorts of groups are important in training the next generation of activists. Young people have designed Christmas cards for sale, taken part in human rights summit meetings, and trained as human rights ambassadors.

Become a cyber activist

You can use your computer and become a cyber activist. The Amnesty International website has information on what is happening around the world in the area of human rights, and shows how you can take part in letter-writing campaigns that could help to save lives. Information and sample letters are available on the Amnesty International site at *www.amnesty.org/*.

Become a volunteer

If you want to be where the action is, you could start volunteering for Amnesty International. Find out where your nearest Amnesty International office is through *www.amnesty.org/* to enquire about local volunteering opportunities. In your next school break, catch a glimpse of how things work, or go in regularly on one or two afternoons each week. There is always something to work on—you may even get to help create new campaigns!

Internet shopping

Even shopping can help. In some countries, and via the Internet, Amnesty International shops sell products to raise money that they use to keep helping people around the world.

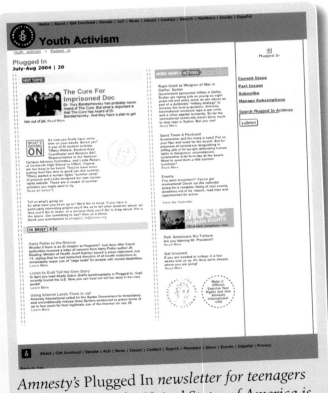

Amnesty's Plugged In *newsletter for teenagers and students in the United States of America is published on the Internet.*

Glossary

activist	a person who takes direct action for a cause
civil war	war between different groups within a country
compensation	money paid for injury or suffering
detention	a type of imprisonment
discriminated	treated unfairly because of race, religion, or other unjust reason
human rights	a set of rights, such as the right to a fair trial, laid down by the United Nations
humanitarian	devoted to people's welfare and the promotion of social reform
lobbying	attempting to convince government, business, or other powerful groups to change their policy or practices
negotiate	discuss, with the aim of reaching an agreement or compromise
Nobel Prize for Peace	an award presented by the Nobel Committee in Sweden to a person or group who gives the greatest benefit to humankind
occupied	taken over and controlled
porters	people employed to carry loads
prisoners of conscience	people who have been put into prison purely for holding beliefs that powerful people disagree with
sentries	people, often military, who watch for intruders
treaty	formal signed agreement between states or countries
unions	associations of workers which fight for better pay and conditions
United Nations	an organization made up of representatives from many countries, that deals with international peace and security
volunteers	people who donate their time to a cause

Index